To Grandma, with Love

Jack Canfield, Mark Victor Hansen

Health Communications, Inc.
Deerfield Beach, Florida

www.hcibooks.com
www.chickensoup.com

Library of Congress Cataloging-in-Publication Data
is available from the Library of Congress

Publisher: Health Communications, Inc.
            3201 S.W. 15th Street
            Deerfield Beach, FL 33442–8190

Cover and inside book design by Larissa Hise Henoch
Photos ©Shutterstock

Grandma,
thank you for
the laughter, the
wonderful stories
and the lessons
you share.

Courtney's Love Lesson

The July day was bursting with sunshine and warmth. The kind of day that whispers, "Let's go to the beach."

Fridays were dear to my heart because Friday was my day to baby-sit our beloved grandchildren, Mikey, three years old, and Courtney, two. Taking them to the beach could only make the day more heavenly. Well . . .

What seemed like a wonderful idea at 10:00 A.M. didn't seem quite so wonderful at 11:00 A.M. as I began unloading the car with all the beach necessities: a blanket, cooler, sand toys, beach towels and two rambunctious toddlers. What in the world had I been thinking? How could I manage all this by myself from the parking lot, which was a city block away from Lake Michigan's edge?

"Dear God, help me," I prayed as I stood there a wee bit overwhelmed, waiting for the morning's estrogen to kick in and calm me down. Just then a group of young, strong men walked by.

"Excuse me," I said. "Would you like to carry some of these things for us? The children are so excited, and I just can't do it all."

The taller of the three, blond and tanned like a California surfer, smiled and answered, "I'd be happy to help. I remember, as a kid, my Gram taking me to the beach."

A short time later, we wished our godsends a happy day as we staked out our homestead a foot from the water's edge and began building a secret tunnel that would take us to Disney World. Mikey was eager to play in the water, splash and "swim," but not Courtney, for the vastness of Lake Michigan and the rolling waves seemed to frighten her. Mikey and I played in the water as Courtney sat in the sand contentedly digging, filling and emptying her pail. No amount of coaxing could persuade her to come into the water.

Suddenly, a strong wind came up, and Gramma's straw beach hat took wings and sailed out across the waves.

"Gram, your hat!" Mikey screamed excitedly.

"I guess it wanted to go swimming, too." We laughed, watching as the waves carried it further out. Then out of the corner of my eye, I saw Courtney step into the water, her little feet taking small, determined steps.

"Court, you're in the water?" Mikey shouted gleefully.

"Me get Gramma's hat," she answered as one little foot was placed in front of the other.

I stood there in the presence of the Lord, who had created this beautiful day, and these grandchildren who lived within my soul, and tears fell from my eyes. Here was a child, so filled with pure love, that her fears were overlooked as she stepped into the water to rescue Gramma's hat.

Scooping Courtney into my arms I whispered, "I love you so much," as we waved good-bye to the beach hat. A five-dollar special at Kmart had taught me a million-dollar lesson.

Alice Collins
Chicken Soup for the Grandparent's Soul

9

Games to Play at the Beach

- Scratch a tic-tac-toe board in the sand with a stick. Just wipe out the board and make a new one when someone wins!

- A classic: Bring buckets and shovels and build sand-castles. Hold contests to see who can build the most elaborate structure.

- Take turns burying each other in the sand. See who can stay under the sand the longest without scratching an itch!

- Bring squirt toys, fill with beach water and squirt each other. (Be careful not to get saltwater in the eyes!)

- Collect shells. Call out instructions such as, "Who can collect the biggest one in one minute?" "Who can find a red one first?" etc.

- Drape a giant beach blanket over the beach umbrella and make a tent!

- Draw pictures or words on each other's backs with sunscreen. Have the person being drawn on guess what's on his or her back.

- Divide into teams of two. Have one person on each team stand at the water's edge and the other stand at the beach blanket. Fill a cup to the brim with beach water and carry it back and forth three times between the two team members. Whichever team has the most water left in the cup at the end of the game wins.

A grandmother
holds her
grandchildren's
hands for a while;
their hearts
forever.

*S*he had the loaded handbag of someone who camps out and seldom goes home, or who imagines life must be full of emergencies.

—Mavis Gallant

Everything but the Kitchen Sink

By my teenage daughters' standards, her purse was huge. Theirs were tiny things that could barely hold a lipstick and compact; they wore them on their shoulders just under their arm. Grandma's handbag, suspended by thick, black leather straps, hung down on her hip. It was big enough to hold everything you could possibly want.

One day we were all in the car when my daughter Shazara spilled some drink on the back seat. "Mom, do you have any napkins?"

"No," I replied.

Suddenly, Grandma reached for her handbag on the car floor near her feet and opened it wide. Her head almost disappeared inside as she rummaged around, pulling out a handful of napkins.

"There you go, sweetheart," she said as she handed them to Shazara.

In my rearview mirror I could see my two daughters sitting there with a huge grins on their faces.

"Mom, there's a thread hanging from my T-shirt," Reece called out.

Again opening the jaws of her handbag, Grandma rummaged in the darkness of her purse and retrieved a pair of scissors.

"There you go, love, " she said, handing it to the girls in the backseat.

They sat with wide grins on their faces that itched with orneriness.

"Mom, I need a knife and fork! " said Shazara, trying hard to sound serious about her request.

Again Grandma opened her bag and her head disappeared into its depths. She handed Shazara a neatly wrapped plastic knife and fork in a white napkin. "Here you are, Shazara."

I could see the girls' faces, looking quite amazed. Surely they weren't going to ask their Grandma for anything else.

"Oh no, my hands are sticky," Reece complained. "Have you got anything that I can wash my hands with, Grandma?"

Again, she delved into the black handbag. I could see the girls waiting in anticipation to see what Grandma was about to produce from her bag this time.

"Here you go," she said, passing a wet tissue in a sealed packet to Reece.

We all laughed out loud when Reece joked, "For a minute, Grandma, I thought you were going to bring out the kitchen sink!"

Nadia Ali

Chicken Soup for the Grandma's Soul

9

What children need
most are the essentials that
grandparents provide in
abundance. They give
unconditional love, kindness,
patience, humor, comfort,
lessons in life. And, most
importantly, cookies.

—Rudolph Giuliani

Nana's Mint Chocolate Chip Cookies

INGREDIENTS:

½ cup brown sugar
½ cup sugar
¾ cup vegetable oil
2 eggs
1 tsp. vanilla
1½ cups flour

1 cup oatmeal
1 tsp baking soda
½ tsp salt
½ cup crushed walnuts
½ cup mint chocolate chips

Preheat oven to 375°.

In a large mixing bowl beat together first five ingredients until creamy. In a separate bowl mix together flour, oatmeal, baking soda and salt. Mix dry ingredients into wet ingredients and add walnuts and mint chocolate chips.

Using a teaspoon, place dollops of cookie dough on an ungreased baking sheet. Flatten using a fork that's been dipped in cold water. Bake at 375° approximately 10 minutes.

Remove from oven and let cool.

Nana's
Mysterious Panache

She was grand! But Nana adamantly disclaimed the title, explaining, "No one is grander than your own mother."

Picture Rosalind Russell's portrayal of Auntie Mame and you get a glimpse of my grandmother. She drove the first car in town, wore pants when that was still scandalous, and she never minded a bawdy joke. Nana dashed through life, lighting up the lives of everyone she met. I wondered why the slings and arrows of life never seemed to overwhelm her.

Basking in the warmth of her sunny presence, I'd watch as the last hairpin was pinned in her brightly hennaed hair. "Want to walk to the grocer's with me, Honeypot?"

"Oh, yes." I was always proud to walk with her. Tall and slender, and dressed so impeccably (she was the only grandmother who wore spike-heeled shoes—an important distinction to me), Nana energetically marched along, calling out, "Hello there, Little Miss Pumpkin. Bunny Boy, how's your lovely mama today?" as neighborhood kids waved and shouted, "Hi, Mrs. K." They sensed here was a woman who knew—and believed—in kids.

Deliverymen and visitors always lingered at Nana's gracious home. Laughing and chattering, she discussed politics or recipes with equal enthusiasm; her gold cigarette holder waving through the air, punctuating the discourse with grace. Framed by a strong, square jaw and prominent cheekbones, her wonderful smile—wrinkles danced as she spoke, and sparkling green eyes watched for signs of trouble. The surly became cheerful; crudeness was treated with gentility. Nana gave strength to the sorrowful, calm to the hysterical, and everyone left feeling touched by her love. Why, I pondered, did she never seem cranky?

Widowed at age fifty-two, she invited me for sleepovers more often. Mornings, waking to her raspy voice singing in the kitchen, brought new adventures in food. "Your breakfast is served, my queen." Pretending to be my lady-in-waiting, Nana pulled out the chair with a flourish. Elegantly set, my place held a juicy, ripe mango and a boiled egg standing in a delicate little cup. Fine crystal and bone china were used daily, never stored away.

Some evenings, after the dinner table was cleared, Nana would throw a sweater over her shoulders and go out into the night. Finally, I asked, "Nana, where are you going . . . can I come?"

"No, darling," she'd chuckle. "This is my alone time." I sensed an air of mystery in this.

One evening, after Nana had slipped out, I climbed out the bedroom window and followed her—at a distance. Nana walked swiftly down two lamplit blocks and went inside the neighborhood church. I hid behind a massive pillar as Nana knelt down in the pew; no prayer book in her hand. After a few moments, she bent her head. When she finally looked up, I saw, in the glimmer of dozens of candles, her face shining with tears. Nana was crying! She stared at the altar. Slowly, ever so slowly, the corners of her mouth began to curve upward. The gentle curve grew and grew. At last, that unique and wonderful smile returned. A moment longer she sat, then, as though consummating a business deal, she briskly arose, genuflected once, and bustled away.

Once back snug in bed, I contemplated what I'd just learned. Bring my sorrows to church. Leave them there. In the face of adversity, put on a smile; before long, it will be genuine. Nana had struggles just like the rest of us; she just refused to succumb to them.

Lynne Zielinski
Chicken Soup for the Grandparent's Soul

Taking joy in living is a woman's best cosmetic.

—Rosalind Russell

Create an Eggshell Garden with Your Grandchildren

Poke a very small hole in the end of a clean eggshell with a toothpick. Fill the shell with dirt and press a few seeds into the dirt. Set the eggshell in a small low box or crate filled with sawdust or some sort of material that will prevent the eggshell from tipping over. Repeat this procedure over and over with different eggshells and different kinds of seeds until your box is full. As you plant each shell, use a marker to write the name of each plant or flower on the eggshell. Children can even carefully decorate their "pots" with colored markers or paints. Place the plants in a sunny window and water as needed. When the plants grow too large for their eggshell homes, gently peel the shells away and replant your "garden" in a larger pot or outdoor garden.

Grandma,
I love you more
than a million
colors!

Grandma's Garden

I watched my grandma hoe the clay soil in my garden.

"Don't see how you grow anything in this," she mused.

"Colorado soil can't compare to yours in Iowa, Grandma!" I stared at her in awe, capturing the moment in my memory forever. Wisps of her silvery hair sneaked from beneath her headscarf as her thin torso bent down to pull a fistful of bindweed.

"This stuff will grow anywhere," she laughed. "Even in this soil!"

Although she lived alone on the Iowa farm she and Grandpa had settled a half-century ago, she still maintained a garden that could sustain most of Benton County! Some of my favorite summer childhood days had been spent in her garden helping her pull up plants she identified as weeds, or planting vegetables and flowers. She had taught me that gardening wasn't only about cultivating plants; it was about cultivating faith. Each seed planted was proof of that. When I was seven I asked, "Grandma, how do the seeds know to grow the roots down and the green part up?"

"Faith," was her answer.

When I grew up and married, my husband recognized the impression Grandma's dirt left under my fingernails and in my heart. He supported my dream to live outside the city, and our two-acre plot had a horse, dog, cat, rabbit, six hens and, of course, a large garden. I was privileged and overjoyed to have Grandma working in it.

Grandma leaned the hoe next to a fence post and walked to my flowerbed to help me plant the lavender plants she'd brought from her garden to mine. She didn't know I was watching as she patted the dirt around the base of a plant. Waving her hand in the sign of a cross above it, she whispered, "God bless you, grow." I'd almost forgotten that garden blessing from my youth. Ten years later, that lavender still flourishes.

Today, I'm a grandmother myself, and my Grandma's lessons still influence me daily. Whenever I tuck a seedling into the earth, I trace a small cross above it in the air and say, "God bless you, grow."

And in quiet times, I can still hear her blessing, nurturing my faith. "God bless you, grow."

LeAnn Thieman
Chicken Soup for the Golden Soul

Lavender

For centuries, lavender has been used both for its aromatic as well as its culinary properties. Along with many other herbs, the Romans introduced lavender to Britain. Queen Victoria is most noted for increasing lavender's popularity as she had it used throughout every room from scenting bed linens, to washing floors and furniture and as an air freshener.

Lavender Sachets

2 cups of lavender leaves
1½ cups of lavender flowers
4 drops of lavender oil

Fabric *(tulle, muslin, organza)*
Needle & Thread
Ribbon

Combine the first three ingredients in a bowl.

Cut your fabric into 8" or 10" circles.

Place 2 tablespoons of the mixed lavender in the center of the circles. Gather the circle and twist closed; using the needle and thread, sew through the twist to keep the material together. Tie off with decorative ribbon.

Afternoon Delight

Mishelle's brown eyes sparkled during the entire ceremony. She couldn't wait for the day she graduated from kindergarten, and had talked about it for weeks. Now she was standing on the stage with her classmates. Twenty five-year-olds wore blue graduation caps with tassels brushing against rosy cheeks flushed with excitement.

I snapped several pictures throughout the morning ceremony, capturing her big smile during each song that had been carefully rehearsed for parents, grandparents and family members. The highlight of the ceremony arrived when my youngest granddaughter marched across the stage to receive her kindergarten diploma.

She is quiet by nature, but I noticed she had little control over the spring in her step, almost skipping to reach her long-awaited certificate. I thought how beautiful she looked in her new pink-and-white flowered dress and patent leather shoes.

Following the ceremony, assorted cookies, frosted cupcakes and red fruity punch was served to the young graduates. While munching on sweets, Mishelle introduced me to several classmates in frilly dresses. Her chatter was excited. And rightly so. This was the biggest day of her life.

Arrangements had been made for the children with working moms to spend the afternoon playing games in a supervised classroom until their parents picked them up. My granddaughter was prepared to join the other children when her mother had to return to work.

I had an idea. Speaking to her mother, I said, "Rather than stay at school, can Mishelle come home with me?"

My daughter-in-law thought for a moment.

"We'll have lunch together," I said, quickly adding, "and you can pick her up after work."

The instant her mother said yes, Mishelle began jumping up and down, clapping her hands.

A passerby, noticing her exuberance, said to Mishelle, "I see you're very excited about graduating today."

"No, not that," she answered.

The bystander looked puzzled, and my heart soared when my granddaughter said, "I'm going to Grandma's house."

Diane M. Vanover

Chicken Soup for the Grandma's Soul

23

All I really need to know about how to live and what to do and how to be I learned in kindergarten.

—Robert Fulghum

Grandma's house is the place where love grows.

We Need a Rock

My mother was in the hospital recovering from a stroke that paralyzed her left side and affected her speech. My sister and I had gone every day to encourage her and try to get her to talk. The doctor said she would speak when she had something to say.

That day, Mom tried to tell me something. Her eyes would look at me and then shoot back to the door. She tried forming the words that her mind was screaming, but her mouth would not cooperate. I knew she was worried about me and wanted me to go home, but I had a month before the baby was due, and I wanted to stay. "I'll be back tomorrow," I finally said, as I waddled out the door. I could see her shaking her head as if to say, "You stay home and rest."

Mom was right. I should have rested. Seven hours later, I was rushed to the emergency room of the same hospital. It was placenta previa. With the help of God and good doctors, I finally lay upstairs from my mother with a beautiful little boy in my arms. As I gazed at him, I kept trying to think of a name. A name is important. A name must have a history that my child can be proud of. But I was too emotionally drained and exhausted to come up with the right one.

Our first son was given his father's name, Daniel. Our second son was given his father's middle name, Michael. Unfortunately, Dan had no more names. Our daughter was named after the most beautiful county in Ireland, Kerry. All the other family names were taken two and three times over by my nephews.

Time was running out; the nurses were pressuring me. I called the nurse and asked her to take a note to my mother on the third floor: "Mom, it's a boy. Will you name him? Love, Kathy."

I waited most of the day for some response. Every time I held the baby, I rocked him and whispered, "Soon you will have a name." All of a sudden, the nurse was standing in the doorway with a mischievous look on her face.

She took the baby and whispered, "Shhh." Startled, I asked, "What's happening?" She motioned for me to get in the wheelchair and be quiet. Another nurse took my baby into the nursery. She wheeled me down a darkened hallway. There in front of the nursery were Dan and my mother, smiling the best crooked smile I ever saw.

"Mom," I called, as the tears welled up in my eyes. This was her first time off the third floor. Then there was a long silence as she raised her left hand and pointed to the nursery where the nurses had brought my baby to the window. In very slow and labored speech, she said, "Name . . . him . . . Peter. We . . . need . . . a rock."

Kathy Ryan
Chicken Soup for the Mother's Soul

When a
baby is born,
so is a
grandma.

If nothing is going well,
call your grandmother!

—Italian proverb

Raising My Sights

My six-year-old granddaughter, Caitlynd, and I stopped at a Tim Horton's donut shop for a blueberry muffin. As we were going out the door, a young teenage boy was coming in.

This young man had no hair on the sides of his head and a tuft of blue spiked hair on top of it. One of his nostrils was pierced, and attached to the hoop that ran through the hole was a chain that draped across his face and attached to a ring he was wearing in his ear. He held a skateboard under one arm and a basketball under the other.

Caitlynd, who was walking ahead of me, stopped in her tracks when she saw the teen. I thought he'd scared the dickens out of her, and she'd frozen on the spot.

I was wrong.

My Grandangel backed up against the door and opened it as wide as it would go. Now I was face to face with the young man. I stepped aside and let him pass. His response was a gracious, "Thank you very much."

On our way to the car, I commended Caitlynd for her manners in holding open the door for the young man. She didn't seem to be troubled by his appearance, but I wanted to make sure. If a grandmotherly talk about freedom of self-expression and allowing people their differences was in order, I wanted to be ready.

As it turned out, the person who needed the talk was me.

The only thing Caitlynd noticed about the teen was the fact

that his arms were full. "He woulda had a hard time to open the door."

I saw the partially shaved head, the tuft of spiked hair, the piercings and the chain. She saw a person carrying something under each arm and heading toward a closed door.

In the future, I hope to get down on her level and raise my sights.

Terri McPherson
Chicken Soup for the Grandparent's Soul

Be not deceived with the
first appearance of things,
for show is not substance.

—English Proverb

Easy Blueberry Muffins

1¾ cups all-purpose flour
⅓ cup sugar
2 tsp. baking powder
¼ tsp. salt
1 beaten egg
¾ cup milk

¼ cup cooking oil
¾ cup fresh or frozen blueberries
1 tsp. finely shredded lemon peel

Preheat oven to 400 degrees F. Mix together the flour, sugar, baking powder and salt. Combine the egg, milk and oil in a separate bowl, then add to the flour mixture. Stir until just moistened. Gently fold blueberries and lemon peel into the batter. Lightly grease muffin cups or use paper liners. Fill cups ⅔ full with batter. Bake about 20 minutes or until muffin tops are golden.

Makes 10 to 12 muffins. Best if served warm!

Thanks

Few things thrill this man more than the sight of my grandmother's handwriting on an envelope. I always save that piece of mail for last, saving it for when I am free to pay it the attention it deserves.

I start with the many enclosures. My grandmother reads at least three newspapers and clips the articles she thinks may be of interest to family members. She prints the newspaper's name and the date the article appeared before folding the clipping so the headline is visible on top.

Today's batch includes a story about another adoptive parent, an announcement about a book signing and tips on defeating kidney stones. I read the clips slowly, knowing that she thought them important enough to send, and her judgment was right on the mark.

Then I finally open my grandmother's card. She buys discounted cards for their pictures and not the printed text, which in this case congratulates me on a new job. The words that matter are the ones she writes herself.

My grandmother starts where most people merely sign their name. She completely fills that page with her neat script, moves over to the facing page, and then finishes her note as the space runs out on the back of the card.

She is thanking me for hosting a birthday party. She doesn't simply say "Thanks," which would still be more than I received from others. My grandmother describes every detail she appreciated, mentions the news she heard and repeats the jokes that made her laugh. She recalls past parties I've thrown and dwells on the highlights.

Those who say that letter writing is a lost art never received mail from my grandmother, who has once again brightened my day and lessened my load.

Stephen D. Rogers
Chicken Soup for the Grandma's Soul

Flowered Thank-you Notes

Good quality paper
Fresh flowers, (small daisies,
   pansies, buttercups, poppies,
   forget-me-nots, clover, etc.)
   delicate fern fronds, or leaves
Coffee filters

Phone book
Scissors
Glue
Tweezers
Small paintbrush

DIRECTIONS:

Place each flower, leaf or frond between two flattened coffee filters and press inside the phone book. (You may also place a couple of bricks on the phone book for added weight.) Allow the flowers to dry for a week or two. (Larger flowers may take longer.)

When dry, remove the flowers from the book and trim off any stems you don't want.

Brush a very thin layer of glue on the paper where you wish to place the flowers. Carefully place the flowers on the glue, using a tweezers if needed to arrange and press down any delicate petals.

Make sure each part of the flowers is touching the glue and lying flat on the paper. Let the glue dry completely.

You now have beautiful stationery or cards.

Grandma,
thanks for always
being there
for me.

Sometimes when we are generous in small, barely detectable ways it can change someone else's life forever.

—Margaret Cho

The Magic Jar Years

One day a mother brought home a small jar and gave it to her little girl on her birthday. She told her little girl that the jar was magic, and she could write to her mommy about anything in the world, put it in the jar, and later, in its place, there would be a note for her. Soon the jar became a special part of their lives.

The little girl loved to get letters from her mommy. They always told her how special she was and had lots of xxxxs and ooos on them. Often there were reminders of something special they had planned together the next day, or a good luck letter if there was a dance recital coming up. Sometimes, too, there would be a little gift in the jar and a note telling her how proud her mommy was of her. She kept all of her mommy's letters in a pretty box by her bed.

The mother treasured each of her little girl's letters, too. There were crayoned "I love yous," tea-party invitations, requests for ballet slippers, and even some Mother's Day cards that had been folded and folded and folded just to fit in the jar. Those always made the mother smile. There was one where her little girl told her she was afraid of the dark, and that very night a small light was placed in her room, and all was well. Another favorite came when their dog Muffin was expecting puppies; there in the jar was a little note that read, "You're going to be a grandma!" The mother kept all of those very special letters safely tucked in a chest at the end of her bed.

As the years went by, that little girl grew into a young lady and then got married and started a home of her own. For the first time, the jar sat empty. The mother dusted the jar every day and sometimes looked inside, remembering—sad that the magic jar years had to end.

One day the young lady came to visit her mother. She went straight to her mother's room, opened the chest at the end of her bed, and found what she was looking for. She folded the piece of paper and put it in the jar, and handed it to her mother. The mother opened the magic jar and there was that note from so long ago, "You're going to be a grandma!"

And when that baby boy was born months later, there was the jar sitting in his nursery with a blue bow tied around it, and a note that read, "Magic jar years never end; they are always just beginning."

Cassie Marie Moore
Chicken Soup for the Mother and Daughter Soul

The Origins of Grandparent's Day

National Grandparent's Day was championed by West Virginia housewife, Marian Lucille Herndon McQuade, as a day for grandchildren to tap into the wisdom and heritage of their grandparents. In 1978, President Jimmy proclaimed that National Grandparent's Day would be celebrated on the first Sunday after Labor Day. The Forget-Me-Not is the official flower of Grandparent's Day.

Where Past and Present, wound in one,
   Do make a garland for the heart:
   So sing that other song I made,
   Half-anger'd with my happy lot,
The day, when in the chestnut shade
   I found the blue Forget-me-not.

—Alfred Lord Tennyson
(excerpted from "The Miller's Daughter")

Gramma, Please Don't Make Me Put Them Back!

When my first granddaughter Lacy was about three or four years old, she was my favorite shopping buddy! I could take her for an afternoon of shopping, and unlike a lot of young children, she never asked for anything.

On one of these shopping outings in early spring, Lacy and I had been in several stores and now we were in a Wal-Mart. As always I had put her in the front of a cart so she could stand and reach all the pretty items. We went up and down several aisles looking at everything. When we got into the children's section, she would reach out, take a dress off the rack and say, "Oh Gramma, isn't this one pretty?" After we both admired it she would hang it back up. This is always how we shopped: We looked, commented, returned the item and moved on. She never asked for these items; she just enjoyed looking at all the pretty things!

We then moved on to the shoe department and as I pushed the cart through the little girls section, she picked up and admired several pairs of shoes. Then she saw a pair of hot pink (pink being her favorite color), high-top suede boots. Slowly reaching for them, she picked them up and cradled them in her arms. Looking up to me, still holding those boots, she said, "Gramma, please don't make me put them back!"

I was surprised with this sudden pleading and asked, "Miss Lacy, what do you need boots for?" After all it was April, winter was over, and it was almost time to start wearing sandals, not boots.

She replied so sadly, "Gramma, they're huntin' boots!" Trying to conceal my laughter, I asked her, "Exactly why do you need huntin' boots?" I knew this dainty, feminine little girl had never gone hunting with Daddy.

She looked at me with an expression that implied God had given her the dumbest of grammas to raise and she said, "For huntin' Easter eggs!"

I'm not sure how another gramma would have handled this situation. I do know Miss Lacy proudly left that store carrying the sack that held her new hot pink huntin' boots!

Karren E. Key

Chicken Soup for the Grandparent's Soul

Famous Grandmothers

Grandma Moses

Rose Kennedy

Granny Smith

Sandra Day O'Connor

Barbara Bush

Queen Elizabeth II

Tina Turner

Phyllis Diller

Lady Bird Johnson

Shirley Jones

Queen Victoria

Birds sing after a storm; why shouldn't people feel as free to delight in whatever sunlight remains to them?

—Rose Kennedy

The Lincoln Zephyr
at Midnight

I was only three years old when my world crumbled.

I knew my mother was sick, but I did not know how seriously ill she really was.

One day a big black car came to our house and took her to a dark, stone hospital high on a hill several miles from home. It was a tuberculosis sanitarium. Daddy could go inside the building, but we children were not allowed to enter. I remember standing by the somber building and looking at a small window high above me. Grandma and Daddy would say, "There's Mama; wave to Mama."

I waved, but all I could see was the faint flutter of a small white hand in the window.

As time went by, my father and grandma decided it was too difficult to maintain our large family, so my three brothers each went to a different family member's home to live. I stayed with Grandma. We traveled all over Iowa. We would stay in someone's home for a few weeks, then Grandma would pack her small black satchel, stow my things in a pillowcase and we'd go someplace else for a while. Thankfully we had a lot of relatives and friends eager to help.

Daddy rented a room near the hospital so he could be near his beloved Gracie. He got a part-time job driving a milk truck. I was bewildered and sad. I did not understand what had happened. Where were my parents? Where were my brothers? And where was my sweet little dog, Jiggs?

Through it all, Grandma was my savior. She comforted me as no one else could. One day we boarded a small train and rode one hundred miles to her son's home by the Mississippi River. What a thrill it was to ride on a real train with Grandma! My uncle met us at the depot and drove us in his Model A to his farm a few miles away. We were happy there. I almost forgot about my real family . . . until around midnight every night.

There was a railroad track across the road from the farmhouse. I loved watching the trains roar by in the daytime. But in the dark of night the mournful wail of the whistle on the sleek new Lincoln Zephyr would waken me as it sped down the tracks. As it faded away into the darkness, I remembered . . . I was in a strange bed, in a strange house, and I didn't know why my family wasn't there.

But Grandma was. She would hold me in her arms and soothe me with her lovely voice until I drifted off to sleep, the sound of the whistle ringing in my ears.

To this day the sound of a train in the darkness takes me back to those lonely nights when I was three, and I still yearn for the comforting, warm arms of my grandmother.

Kathryn Kimzey Judkins
Chicken Soup for the Grandma's Soul

Travel

The railroad track is miles away,
And the day is loud with voices speaking,
Yet there isn't a train goes by all day
But I hear its whistle shrieking.

All night there isn't a train goes by,
Though the night is still for sleep and dreaming,
But I see its cinders red on the sky,
And hear its engine steaming.

My heart is warm with friends I make,
And better friends I'll not be knowing;
Yet there isn't a train I'd rather take,
No matter where it's going.

Edna St. Vincent Millay

Home is where grandma is.

A home without a
grandmother is like an
egg without salt.

—Florence King

Love gives naught but itself and takes naught but from itself. Love possesses not nor would it be possessed; For love is sufficient unto love.

—Kahlil Gibran

Becoming a Grandma

After three days of labor, my daughter Déjà had her first child, a beautiful seven-pound four-ounce girl. I was amazed to observe that the instant she saw her new baby, the pain of childbirth was immediately replaced by the bliss of motherhood.

In those first few heart-stopping minutes of becoming a grandmother, one particular moment stands out for me. A moment set apart from everything else that was happening by the sudden depth of our connection—daughter, mother and grandmother.

My beautiful daughter turned to me, her eyes shining with a light I had never seen there before. "Mom," she said, "now I know how much you love me."

Robin Lim
Chicken Soup for the Mother's Soul 2

*P*erfect love sometimes
does not come until the first
grandchild.

—Welsh Proverb

A World of Love

Ti voglio bene (Italian)

Ich liebe dich (German)

Je t'aime (French)

Wo ie ni (Chinese)

Te amo (Spanish)

Volim te (Croatian)

Eu te amo (Protuguese)

Miluji te (Czech)

Jeg elsker dig (Danish)

S' agapo (Greek)

Ta gra agam ort (Gaelic)

Seni seviyorum (Turkish)

Szeretlek te'ged (Hungarian)

Ikh hob dikh lib (Yiddish)

Kimi o ai shiteru (Japanese)

Twenty-Nine and Holding

Our family had always been big on birthday celebrations and other special occasions. On each and every birthday, my entire family gathered together to share a meal, gifts and a song. My mother wasn't fond of her own birthdays. Like many women her age, when her birthday rolled around she only admitted to being twenty-nine, just as she was the year before.

At the ripe old age of twelve, my twin sons had figured out that Grandma was much older than she admitted, but didn't question her when she once again announced that she was twenty-nine and holding. My younger daughter, Becky, took her seriously, however. She believed every word that her grandmother told her. If Grandma said she was twenty-nine, as far as Becky was concerned, she was twenty-nine. There was no question about it.

A few months went by, and we joined together as a family to celebrate my thirtieth birthday. After everyone sang "Happy Birthday," we enjoyed heaping helpings of cake and ice cream. Finally, the time came for me to open my presents. Becky had been unusually quiet during the entire birthday celebration. She carried a worried look on her face.

After all of the guests left, she couldn't stand it any longer and sadly informed me, "Mamma, you're thirty, and Grandma is twenty-nine. I hate to have to tell you this, but you must've been adopted."

Nancy B. Gibbs
Chicken Soup for the Grandparent's Soul

The secret of staying young is to live honestly, eat slowly, and lie about your age.

—Lucille Ball

A mother becomes a true grandmother the day she stops noticing the terrible things her children do because she is so enchanted with the wonderful things her grandchildren do.

—Lois Wyse

Creative Gift Wrapping Ideas

- Shop fabric stores for sales on fabric remnants and ribbon to wrap your gifts in! Top with "corsages" of silk or plastic flowers from the craft or dollar store.

- Wrap your packages in gold or silver foil. Tie with an elegant ribbon.

- Use the comic pages from the Sunday newspaper. (Make sure they're in color!) Kids are especially fond of having their gifts wrapped in "the funnies."

- Top kids' gifts with items they can play with, such as plastic animals, whistles, pencils and toy cars. Use colorful shoelaces on boys' gifts. Fasten ribbon with barrettes that little girls can wear!

- Tie tubes of lip gloss or lipstick onto women's packages. Adorn men's packages with tubes of lip balm or fishing lures!

- Wrap gifts in plain brown paper, then use decorative rubber stamps and colorful inks to decorate your packages!

• Use a scarf or a bandanna to wrap a present . . . your recipient will appreciate the extra gift!

• Recycle old wall calendars with colorful pictures as gift wrap. Of course, don't forget to wrap with the picture side "up"!

• Wrap your gifts in white paper, then let the grandkids get out their paints or crayons and decorate! Show them how to accessorize with glitter, buttons or beads.

• Place your gifts in a decorative basket that the recipient can reuse.

*C*hildren are the keys
of paradise.

—Richard Henry Stoddard

Start Your Own "Star" Tradition

Keep in touch with your grandchildren by starting your own "Star of the Week" tradition. If you have only a few grandchildren, change it to the "Star of the Month." Each month, send the chosen child a special award certificate saying, "You've been selected as Grandma's Star of the Month!" Include star-shaped confetti and small gifts. Call or e-mail the recipient to congratulate him or her. If you live close by, take the "star" out for ice cream, a movie or a special meal. Send a special card every day or week. Your grandchildren will love this new family tradition!

Star of the Week

Joyce and Morgan Ilgenfritz are grandparents to twenty grandchildren. Fifteen in one family live in Pennsylvania, less than two hours from them. Two live in Colorado and the other three in West Africa.

Joyce and Morgan have also housed 370 people in their home over the last thirty years. In addition to those who are presently living with them, they are caring for Morgan's ninety-year-old mother, who has Alzheimer's disease. So their days are full.

Next to her relationship with the Lord, Joyce's top priority is her grandchildren. She is on the lookout year round for gifts and cards, and never waits until an occasion arrives to prepare for it. But she would be the first to admit that staying in touch takes some creativity.

Recently, Joyce was pondering what more she could do.

"I was in a store right after Valentine's Day," she explains, "and saw a picture frame and two heart boxes. They were reduced in price, but I didn't buy them. That night," she continues, "I had a conversation with God. 'Lord, I have all these grandchildren,'" I said. "'How can I stay connected with them?'"

Joyce drifted off to sleep and soon awoke with a clear direction from the Lord. "He said to go back to the store and get the frame and boxes," she recalls. "Then he told me what to do with them."

Joyce could hardly wait for morning. She went to the store, made the purchase and placed the items on her kitchen windowsill. Then she collected pictures of each of her grandchildren and wrote all their names on pieces of paper, which she placed in one of the boxes.

Now each week she draws a name from the first box, puts that child's picture in the frame, and places the name in the second box for the next time around. That child is her "Star of the Week."

Immediately, she calls (e-mails to Africa) and informs the star of his or her status. Then she asks for prayer requests. The child gleefully anticipates hearing from her again during the week by way of another phone call, a letter or a package—or possibly all three.

Recently, five-year-old Moriah hung up from his phone call and announced loudly to any of his fourteen brothers and sisters within hearing distance, "I'm Grandma's Star of the Week!"

When six-year-old Ashley got her call, she told her grandma there was a girl in her class who was saying mean things about her.

"You just be nice to her and I'll be praying," Joyce responded.

The next time her grandma called, Ashley said, "That little girl has been so nice to me, and I know it's because you've been praying."

Being Star of the Week not only makes twenty grandchildren happy, it fulfills the desire of their grandma's heart, allowing her to focus on one grandchild at a time, to pray specifically for that child's needs, and to surprise the "Star" with gifts of love.

Bonnie S. Grau
Chicken Soup for the Grandma's Soul

Tradition means that we need to end what began well and continue what is worth continuing."

—Jose Bergamin

Famous TV and Big Screen Grandmothers

June Monsoon–Absolutely Fabulous

Endora–Bewitched

Daisy Moses–The Beverly Hillbillies

Dorothy Zbornak–The Golden Girls

Queen Clarisse Renaldi—The Princess Diaries

Esther "Grandma" Walton—The Waltons

Emily Gilmore—The Gilmore Girls

Marie Barone—Everybody Loves Raymond

Grandmama Addams—The Addams Family

Grandma Lois

A few years ago my husband and I were riding in the car with our friends Denny and Laurie Montgomery and Grandma Lois, Denny's mother. Having known the family for years, we were always braced for whatever Lois would say. She was about seventy-five at that time . . . somewhat hard of hearing, but alert and spunky as anything. Driving through an older part of North Seattle, we passed some weathered brick buildings that had advertisements and pictures painted on the sides of them. Coming up on our right was an old-fashioned eye clinic or something . . . an optometrist's office, probably. On the side of the building was a graphic painting of a gigantic eye with very special details—the pupil, iris, eyelashes. . . .

Lois barked out from the back seat: "DENNY, WHAT IS THAT!?"

"On that building, you mean? It's a picture of an eye, I think, Mom."

"WHAT is it? A picture of what?"

"It's an EYE, Mom . . . a picture of an eye."

This irritated Lois for some reason . . . a giant picture of an eye evidently didn't sit right with her. She seemed to find it ridiculous and annoying.

"Well! (tsk!) An EYE?! Why on Earth would anybody paint an EYE like that on a building!?" She rolled her eyes and abruptly crossed her arms.

Denny loved Lois dearly, and he never seemed to tire of her cynical nature. He was patient no matter what was bothering her, and something usually was.

"Well, the guy's probably an eye doctor, Mom, and that's his advertisement. It's probably an optometrist's office, or something. Maybe he's an optician."

"Well for heaven's sake!" Lois sniffed, thoroughly disgusted. "Humph!" She was shaking her head. "Aren't ya' just glad he wasn't a gynecologist!!!?"

Patricia S. Mays
Chicken Soup for the Grandparent's Soul

Is not wisdom found among the aged? Does not long life bring understanding?

—Job 12:12

Grandma, your sense of humor brings light into my life.

A grandma's hugs are the best hugs there are.

A grandmother pretends
she doesn't know who you are
on Halloween.

—Erma Bombeck

Little Marie

I have a great brood of grown children, many who have scattered to the far corners. We call frequently, and I send letters stuffed with coupons for diapers, baby food and things. In return, Papa and I get sent silly pictures of our growing grandchildren or crayon drawings done in school.

We love the photos and the artwork, but miss being able to go to their soccer games, dance recitals and birthday parties.

Last summer we planned a large family reunion. Finally, we'd be able to gather all our wonderful grandchildren together.

Our youngest son arrived with our youngest granddaughter. Marie was three with chubby cheeks just begging to be pinched. My daughter-in-law, well-meaning as she was, pushed Marie toward us. "Give Grandma and Grandpa kisses hello," she said.

Marie looked panicked and ducked behind her mom's legs. She held on tightly despite our daughter-in-law's urges to give us a hug and kiss. After a moment, I said that maybe Marie would like to kiss us another time, when she was more familiar with us. Our daughter-in-law, embarrassed, agreed that this might be better.

Throughout the reunion week Marie continued to hide whenever her mom asked her to give us a kiss. It pained me that my own granddaughter was afraid of me. Marie's behavior reinforced the loneliness I felt from being so far away from my children and grandchildren.

The week came to an end, and our son prepared to leave for the airport. I knew my daughter-in-law would try one final time to get Marie to kiss us. I wanted our good-byes to be happy so I decided to try something different.

Before my daughter-in-law could insist upon a kiss, I told her that I needed to say a special good-bye to Marie.

I bent over and stared right into Marie's eyes. We stared good and long until finally I had to stand up.

"What was that all about?" asked my son.

Still looking at Marie's pensive little face I said, "Our eyeballs kissed."

Slowly, Marie's face began to transform. A grin split from ear to ear and she laughed. Then she ran to me and gave me a big hug. "Silly Gramma," she whispered in my ear.

"I'll miss you."

We'll miss her, too.

Angela D'Valentine
Chicken Soup for the Grandparent's Soul

Tips for a Successful Family Reunion

• Form a committee of dedicated family members so the burden of planning the reunion doesn't fall on one person. Make a to-do list and divide it among the committee members.

• Announce the reunion far in advance of the date so that family members can reserve the time before other activities arise. This also gives people time to make travel arrangements and save money in case they need to travel.

• For small reunions, backyard barbecues or park picnics are inexpensive and fun. Assign everyone a type of dish to bring so that you don't end up with twenty desserts and only one main course. Don't forget condiments, cups/plates/silverware and drinks!

• If the reunion is to be at a hotel, call about getting a group discount. Many hotels will offer rooms at reduced rates if a certain number of rooms are reserved. Make sure the hotel is reasonably priced for everyone.

- Hold an auction or raffle at your reunion to help pay for the event. It's a fun activity, too!

- Create handouts such as a family recipe book or a photo album. Have family members send in recipes or photos well in advance of the event and have them put together into a book, making enough copies for each family.

- Do special events for the kids. Hold hula-hoop or pie-eating contests; set up water slides; put up a volleyball net, etc.

- Take lots of pictures and put them on a Web site when the reunion is done so that everyone can "revisit" the festivities.

- Make up "family T-shirts" or hats for everyone to wear.

- Videotape the event. Interview each family and have them give a special message. Sell the videos for a reasonable price after the event.

Dinner Out

We went to a little cafe
  just off the campus
  to have a quiet dinner together,
the college students there
  eating, discussing deep philosophical issues.

You sat at our table
  looking suave and debonair in jeans and turtleneck,
  your tousled hair shining,
  your eyes sparkling, full of mischief.
And you worked your charms
  on me and everyone around.

The waitress doted on you,
  your cup always filled
"An extra napkin? Certainly!"
"More crackers for your soup? Of course!"
You flirted notoriously with her
  and with the hostess as well,
  flashing seductive grins at them,
  inviting them to talk,
  eating only the fringes of your meal.

Twice you left our table
    to walk around
    and spread your charms elsewhere,
    stopping at a table or two,
    grinning broadly, flirtatiously,
    soliciting conversation.
I watched you captivate their hearts
    and knew you had taken mine,
    as I sat quietly observing.

Finally, folding my dinner napkin patiently
    and placing it beside my finished plate,
I knew it was time to go,
and walking up to you I said,
    "Let's say good-bye."

And picking you up, I placed you
    in your stroller,
    and as we left,
you waved profusely at everyone,
after your first dinner out with Grandma,
    when you were only two.

Maryann Lee Jacob
Chicken Soup for the Mother's Soul

Grandma's Recipe for Happiness

2 heaping cups of patience
1 heart full of love
2 hands full of generosity
dash of laughter
1 head full of understanding
Sprinkle generously with kindness
Add plenty of faith and mix well.
Spread over a period of a lifetime
And serve to everyone you meet.

A grandmother is a little bit parent, a little bit teacher, and a little bit best friend.

One Finger

"Mom, you should put some of your things away. Baby-proof this house," stated our oldest son Mark as he lumbered up the stairs followed by his wife, Kim, and fifteen-month-old Hannah.

Visiting for the Thanksgiving holiday, he finished unloading the luggage and took it to the guest room downstairs. After driving all day from Salt Lake to Ft. Collins, his temper showed.

"That one-finger rule may work with the twins, but it'll never work with Hannah," he insisted.

When my three granddaughters were born four months apart and the twins moved into our house at eight months, my close friend offered me her secret to entertaining grandchildren with few mishaps.

"Teach them the 'one-finger rule.'" All of her five grandchildren learned it at a young age. The success of the method surprised me.

I picked up my granddaughter and said, "Well, Mark, you just watch." I hugged her and walked all around the great room.

"Hannah, you may touch anything in this room you want. But, you can only use one finger."

I demonstrated the technique by touching my forefinger to the African sculpture on the mantel. Hannah followed my example.

"Good girl. Now what else would you like to touch?"

She stretched her finger toward another object on the mantel. I allowed her to touch everything in sight—plants, glass objects, TV, VCR, lamps, speakers, candles and artificial flowers. If she started to grab, I gently reminded her to use one finger. She always obeyed.

But Hannah, an only child, possessed a more adventurous personality. Her father predicted it would prevent her from accepting the one-finger rule.

During their four-day stay, we aided Hannah in remembering the one-finger rule. She learned quickly. I only put away the things that might prove to be a danger to a child. Otherwise, we watched her closely, and nothing appeared to suffer any damage. Besides, "things" can be replaced.

A few fingerprints on glass doors, windows and tables remained after Hannah and her family returned home. I couldn't bring myself to clean them for days. Each one reminded me of some wonderful experience with Hannah.

Months later, my husband and I drove to Salt Lake, and I watched Mark and Kim continue to practice the one-finger rule. But I refrained from saying, "I told you so." Yet, I smiled inwardly each time they prodded Hannah to touch with "one finger."

Mark, a salesman, always gave a packet of gifts to his potential clients. The night before we returned home, Mark sat on the floor stuffing gifts into their packets.

Hannah helped.

Then she picked up one gift, held it in her hand as if it were a fragile bird, and walked toward me. At my knee, her beautiful blue eyes looked into mine. She stretched her prize to me and said, "One finger, Nana!"

Linda Osmundson
Chicken Soup for the Grandparent's Soul

How to Baby-Proof Your House

- Lock up all medicines, vitamins and pills.

- Place cleaners and detergents out of children's reach.

- Make sure there are no small objects around that babies can swallow.

- Scan the room for sharp objects and remove them from baby's reach.

- Place covers on all electrical outlets.

- Move all electrical and extension cords out of reach.

- Keep children away from fans and space heaters.

- Put latches on dresser drawers and cupboards.

- Place tight covers on trashcans and diaper pails.

- Keep the toilet lid down.

- Be sure to cushion the sharp corners and edges of furniture.

- Avoid using any toy chest or container with a hinged lid that can fall and hurt children.

- Get down on your hands and knees for a "child's-eye view" of dangers in the environment.

- If a pet is unaccustomed to children, place him in a separate room until you've determined he won't harm the child. Never leave a child unattended with an animal.

Digging in the Dirt

"Dig in the dirt with me, Noni."

My three-year-old grandson, Ethan, stood in the kitchen with pleading eyes and a big spoon. I had two large clay pots with soil that needed changing, and he needed something to do—a perfect match. After getting the necessary digging utensil from the junk drawer, he'd rushed to the deck and sent dirt flying everywhere. I could just imagine my daughter's reaction to his dirty clothes, but that was okay with me. As the grandma, I'm allowed to spoil.

It was hard to resist his invitation to play, but I had a meeting that night and I still had to fix supper.

"I can't right now, honey. Noni's busy."

Ethan hung his head and stared at his shoes all the way back outside. Guilt hovered over me while I chopped celery and onions for meatloaf. Some grandma! But, I reasoned, it's different being a grandmother these days. I'm younger, busier. I don't have time to play like mine did when I was a child.

As I watched Ethan through the window, memories of a tea party with my grandmother surfaced. I remembered how Mammie filled my blue plastic teapot with coffee-milk and served toasted pound cake slathered in butter. She carried the tray as we walked to the patio and sat under the old magnolia tree that was full of fragrant, creamy-white blooms. I served the cake, poured the coffee into tiny plastic cups and stirred with an even tinier spoon. Our playtime probably lasted less than thirty minutes, and yet, after all these years, I still remembered.

Ethan saw me watching him and pointed to the pot. He had emptied it. I waved and nodded to him. Just then it dawned on me that my love for flowers came from Mammie. She had dug in the dirt with me. I recalled the new bag of potting soil and flower seeds I had in the garage. It would be fun to plant seeds and watch them grow with my little grandson.

I left my knife on the chopping block, found another old spoon and went outside.

"Noni can play now."

Ethan clapped his dirty hands as I plopped down beside him. What fun we had that sunny afternoon. Supper was on time, and so was I for my meeting.

I learned the important life secret that Mammie always knew: There's always time to play.

Linda Apple

Chicken Soup for the Grandma's Soul

Granny Smith Apple Pie

Pastry for 2 pies
6 cups cored, peeled and
   sliced Granny Smith apples
1 cup packed brown sugar
2 tablespoons flour
1 tablespoon lemon juice

1 teaspoon cinnamon
¼ teaspoon nutmeg
1 tablespoon butter
milk
sugar

PREPARATION:

Preheat oven to 425°. Put bottom crust in pie pan. In a large bowl, mix all other ingredients together, except the butter, milk and sugar. Pour the mixture into crust and dot with butter.

Place remaining pie crust on top and flute edges with a fork.

Cut vents in top crust. Using a pastry brush, paint the top crust with milk and sprinkle with sugar. Bake for 15 minutes. Remove from oven and cover outside edge of crust with aluminum foil. Finish baking pie for an additional 25 to 30 minutes.

Granny Smith

Maria Ann Sherwood was born in Sussex, England in 1799. At the age of 19, she married Thomas Smith and in 1838 they emigrated to New South Wales with their five children.

Like many in New South Wales, Thomas and Maria were orchadists, and they specialized in growing many of their own varieties of fruit, including seedling apples.

In a 1924 interview, Edwin Small, a local fruit grower, recalled that in 1868 Maria Smith had invited him and his father to view a seedling apple that was growing by a creek on her property. She explained that the seedling had been developed from the remains of some French crab apples grown in Tasmania.

Although they never became a commercial variety in Maria's lifetime, Granny Smith apples are one of the most popular varieties in supermarkets today.

Gran

When I was a young mother my grandmother, who was lonely after my grandfather's death, visited me every month for a few days. We'd cook together and talk, and she'd always babysit, so I could have time to myself.

By the time she was ninety-five, practically deaf and very frail, I was working part-time, and two of my three children were in school. Gran would come to our home on days when I wasn't working. Once when she was visiting, my older children were in school, my eighteen-month-old was sleeping, and Gran and I were having coffee. I always felt protected and relaxed when we were together.

Then I got a telephone call that there was a crisis in my office—would I please come in for an hour or two. Gran assured me that she and Jeff, the eighteen-month-old, would be fine, and I left.

As I drove to work, I panicked. I'd left my deaf, elderly grandmother with an eighteen-month-old she was not strong enough to pick up and could not hear if he cried. But Gran inspired so much confidence that I felt it would be all right. And perhaps, if I was lucky, my son would sleep the whole time I was gone.

I returned two hours later and heard happy sounds coming from Jeff's room. He'd awakened, she'd dragged a chair next to his crib, and she was reading him a story. He sat there, enchanted by her voice, unperturbed by the bars of the crib that separated them. And our German shepherd lay at her feet, also completely content.

The drama of that day did affect Gran, who later admitted that communicating with an eighteen-month-old presented some problems. Unlike adults, if he'd needed something and wanted her to know about it, of course he couldn't write it down. The next week she enrolled in a lip-reading course at a local college. The teacher was a young intern, and Gran was her only student. After the first session, the teacher made the trip to Gran's apartment each week, so Gran wouldn't have to travel to the college, changing buses twice. By the end of the semester, Gran's ability to lip-read had greatly improved, and she felt infinitely more comfortable with Jeff and with the rest of the world.

Mary Ann Horenstein
Chicken Soup for Every Mom's Soul

Grandma,
you inspire me
to be a better
person.

That is happiness; to be dissolved into something complete and great.

—Willa Cather

The Bathroom Mirror

As I approach the bathroom mirror, I cautiously scrutinize the reflection staring back at me. I have recently been given a new name: "Grandma."

I brace myself against the counter while squinting my eyes at the face in the mirror. How could this woman possibly be a grandmother? She looks nothing like the grandmother of my childhood. This woman doesn't have a speck of gray in her hair. And there is not a trace of wrinkles or age spots to be seen. Of course, to be fair, my grandmother didn't have fifty different boxes of hair coloring conveniently awaiting her at the store or the wonderful selection of anti-aging creams that line my counter like good little soldiers. Still it is difficult to believe that I have earned this title of "Grandma."

Where have the years gone? My mind wanders back to my own childhood. I did have a very nice childhood, nothing out of the ordinary. However, I do remember certain phrases my mother used that I swore would never pass through my lips. I still gasp in horror when I remember uttering for the first time to my kids, "It's always fun and games until somebody gets hurt!" I swear, my head did a ninety-degree turn to see if my mother was standing nearby. Had those words really come from my mouth? Those were my mother's words. I was possessed! And the first time I heard my mother's laugh coming out of my throat, it was almost as if a full moon was turning me into a werewolf. I was downright quivering with fear.

Then there's the memory when I was eight years old, storming down the hall toward my bedroom in a snit over one of my mom's judgment calls. I slammed the door behind me with all my strength, purging my rage. Mom appeared within seconds, demanding to know why I slammed the door. Being blessed with very large eyes that could widen to angelic heights, I softly whimpered, "It was the wind, Mama. See, the window is open." It worked like a charm—and it still worked when my kids used it on me.

There's something about the word "mama" when spoken by a child that has the power to unleash a force so strong that it can turn a mother's heart into quivering Jell-O. As I stand before the mirror this morning, I ponder what the word "Grandma" will do to me. I envision a huge bowl of mush with the words, "Help me, I'm drowning," written on top in brown sugar with two large eyes blinking through it.

How has my childhood blurred into my children's childhood and now into their children's childhood? Where has the time gone? I realize the answer is gazing back at me in the mirror. It is within me. It is in my spirit and within my heart. I have become my mother and, in turn, a grandmother. I no longer quake in fear over the transition. I embrace it with a smile. This girl, this mother and now this grandmother is going to be just fine.

Wanda Mitchell

Chicken Soup for the Grandparent's Soul

Wrinkles should merely indicate where smiles have been.

—Mark Twain

Grandma,
thinking of you
always gives my
heart a lift!

By Any Other Name

Contemplating my impending role as grandparent, I spent countless hours and multiple conversations debating what my new grandchild should call me. After all, this was a big decision: a sacred moniker—set in stone—to be used by countless future grandchildren.

I mused over the merits and disadvantages of various names, rolling them around my tongue, tasting them, savoring them—trying them on for size. *Grandmother?* Too formal. *Grandma?* Mundane. *Nana?* Nah.

From the quirky *Punkin'* to the colloquial *Gran*, the whimsical *Oma* to the formal *Grandma-ma* (with an elegant accent on the last syllable), I experimented with them all.

"Give it up," said my more experienced girlfriends. "That first grandbaby will call you what she will. And, anyway, the actual name won't matter. Why, you'll be so thrilled, it won't matter *what* she calls you. Trust us," they nodded in agreement. "You won't care."

Well, grandbaby Avery turned one and my daughter put her on the phone so I could hear her chatter across the two thousand miles separating us. I knew this verbose babe's burgeoning repertoire now included words like drink, ball, banana, hi and even the names of several animals. With any luck . . .

"Hello, sweet pea," I gushed. "Happy birthday!"

"Avery, say 'hi' to Grammy," my daughter coaxed at the other end. "Say 'hi.'"

And then it happened. It really happened. A precious, breathy little voice pulled together two words from her vocabulary and cooed into the phone, "Hi, dog."

My daughter giggled, then erupted into a full laugh—and baby Avery repeated her new achievement with enthusiasm, delighted that it appeared to make her mommy so happy.

"Hi dog, hi dog, hi dog."

Huh, I laughed, my girlfriends were wrong. I care. I care *a lot*.

Carol McAdoo Rehme
Chicken Soup for the Grandma's Soul

Grandma, by
any other name…

Abuela

Abuelita

Bubbe

G'ma

Gamma

Gammy

Gams

Gannie

Gommy

Gram

Gramma

Grammy

Grams

Gran

Grandmama

Grandmom

Granny

Mamaw

Mawmaw

Meemaw

Meme

Mom-Mom

Nai Nai

Nana

Nanny

Noni

Nonna

Oma

Ya Ya

Gift from Another Grandmother

Our son, Bob, placed a little stranger down in the middle of our living room. "Mom, Dad, this is my Bridget." Bridget, two and a half, stood there and just smiled, her hazel-brown eyes dancing from one of us to the other. She had been born in the northernmost part of Canada where the aurora borealis can be seen from her yard. This was her first trip to Washington State, and she took my breath away.

We hugged and laughed and greeted one another, then I asked if Bridget would like to help me in the yard. We gathered all the tools, and as I knelt in the pansy beds beneath our birch trees, Bridget wiggled her plump body close. "Grandma, are you allowed to get dirty?"

"You bet. And so are you."

The next morning we threw our sleeping bags and groceries into the trucks and headed for the ocean. Bridget sat straight and tall between her grandfather and me. As we started off down the driveway, she smiled up at me and carefully took my arm, cradling it between both of her chubby hands, and just hung on for two hundred miles.

Bridget had learned the word, "Grandma," from our daughter-in-law's mother, who lived near their homestead. So we didn't need time to get acquainted. "Run, Grandma, run," Bridget called as we held hands, lifted our faces to the wind and ran toward the ocean waves. She giggled and splashed as the sun and surf painted rainbows across our toes at the water's edge.

That night Bridget never left my side as we toasted marshmallows, our cheeks and fingers melding together with traces of white, sticky sweetness. At bedtime, she rolled out her bag and put it on the canvas floor beside my old army surplus cot in our nine- by nine-foot tent. Grandpa was already snoring and the other grandchildren chose to sleep under the stars with Uncle Brian. As Bridget and I talked about taking our pails to the beach in the morning, she lifted my hand to her lips, "Grandma 'Rean says you're nice." And we drifted off to dreams as the auspicious drone of waves and shifting sand washed across our world.

In the middle of the night a noise awakened me. And in the faint, first light of morning through the tent screen flap, I saw Bridget sit up in her bag and lean onto my cot. She reached across my stomach and hugged me, then brushed her lips across my cheek. Very carefully she patted my arm. Then she scooted back inside the Mickey Mouse bag, closed her dark lashes and snuggled her ponytail into the pillow.

I caught my breath and lay very still, allowing warm tears to wash the memory of Bridget's visit deep into my bones. I held a treasure: my grandchild's ready, open heart, the gift of Grandma Mearean, up north nearly two thousand miles away.

Doris Hays Northstrom
Chicken Soup for the Grandparent's Soul

S'Mores

large marshmallows
chocolate candy bars
graham crackers

Toast marshmallows on a stick or skewer over a grill or campfire until the sides are golden brown.

Place a piece of chocolate on top of a graham cracker section. Top with the toasted marshmallow (once it's cool enough to touch!). Top with another graham cracker section and press down.

Enjoy!

Relaxing Moments

- Take a nice long walk

- Watch a funny movie or TV show

- Take a hot bubble bath surrounded with scented candles.

- Soak your feet

- Listen to relaxing music

- Arrange a pretty bouquet of flowers

- Read a Good book

- Trim the roses

You must learn to be still in the midst of activity and to be vibrantly alive in repose.

—Indira Gandhi

A grandmother is a mother who has a second chance.

—Author Unknown

The Feeling

I sat in a beautiful city park one day watching my three-year-old granddaughter swinging when I felt this take-your-breath-away feeling. It was a feeling I had often experienced on our own little piece of land out in the country.

It is strange how we ended up buying that place. We were looking for a place to live and finally discovered an old farmhouse on an acre and a half thirty minutes from the city. The house had been built as a one-room schoolhouse in 1911, and the basement was still a dirt cellar. Looking at this old place, I regretted the thought of giving up my beautiful home in the city, with wall-to-wall carpets, a lovely fireplace and a bay window. I knew my husband wanted a country place, but giving up my city home was not going to be easy. Then we walked out across the land, and this beautiful feeling hit me. I commented to my husband, "It feels so good here."

We looked through the old place and once again walked out in the yard, and as we traveled down a wee slope to a tree-lined enclosure this wondrous feeling again came upon me. "Honey, it feels so good here!" I guess I told him that at least three or four times that day and again in the weeks and months that followed our purchase of the home. I received that glorious feeling each time I walked into a small enclosure we called our Secret Garden.

But I was not the only one to feel this warm energy. Each time we had company, I encouraged them to spend some time alone in the Secret Garden, and every single person said the same thing. They felt a good, warm feeling come over them.

Now here I was in a park with my granddaughter and I had that same amazing feeling. I called to my rambunctious little granddaughter, "Jani, come over here and sit with Grandma."

She climbed up on the park bench and managed to slow her energetic little body long enough to listen. "Jani, will you sit here with me and just close your eyes and see if you feel anything?"

Bless her; she didn't question my weird request. She merely closed her eyes and sat perfectly still. I waited to see if she would experience what I did. And then I kept on waiting, as she seemed in no hurry to open her eyes. This was surprising for such a lively little bundle of energy.

Finally I could wait no longer. "Jani?" I touched her shoulder, gently encouraging her to open her eyes. As she did, I asked her, "Jani, did you feel anything?"

She beamed a beautiful, radiant smile and said, "Oh Gamma, it felt like God giving me a hug!"

Ellie Braun-Haley
Chicken Soup for the Grandma's Soul

Grandma,
you're in my
thoughts . . .
today and always.

A hug delights and warms
and charms, that must be why
God gave us arms.

—Source Unknown

Just One Wish

Colby Point was the name of a road that crept between the hills and valleys of McHenry, Illinois. At the very end of the road three houses faced one another. Three sisters—all single seniors—lived in one of the homes. Across the way their widowed cousin lived in a yellow house. Next to her lived their brother, Bill, and his wife, Cleo.

Cleo had multiple sclerosis, so the pair had moved to Colby Point seeking a quiet, relaxed life. Little did they know that they would end up rearing their granddaughter, Margie. The once-quiet neighborhood became active with the sounds of a child.

Margie always looked forward to Christmas, and this year was no different. Everyone was in a flurry, for at the church Margie and her family attended, the congregation was preparing to share their Christmas wishes. Since Cleo couldn't make it to church, and Bill didn't like to leave her alone for long, he was in the habit of dropping Margie off at church early on Sundays; the aunts would bring her home.

As Margie sat in church that morning, she rehearsed in her mind over and over what she would say. One after another, the church members shared their wishes. Margie was the last and the youngest to speak, "I would like for my grandma to have church. She cannot walk, and she and my grandpa have to stay home. They miss coming so much. And please don't tell them, for it needs to be a surprise."

Riding home with her aunts, Margie could tell they were

speaking in low tones about her wish. She hoped that they would keep her secret. As the next Sunday came around, Margie was getting ready for church when Grandma asked, "Why are you so fidgety?"

"I just know that something wonderful is going to happen today!"

"Of course it will," her grandma chuckled. "It's almost Christmas."

Grandpa was getting on his coat when he looked out the front window. He saw some cars coming down the dirt road one after another. Now at this time of year there wasn't too much traffic, so this was really amazing. Margie pushed her grandma to the window so she could see. Pretty soon the cars were parked up and down the road as far as a person could see.

Grandpa looked at Grandma, and they both looked at Margie. Grandpa asked, "Just what did you wish for, Margie?"

"I wished that you and Grandma could have church. I just knew that it would come true. Look! There's the pastor, and everyone from church is coming."

The congregation arrived with coffee and cookies, cups and gifts. They sang carols and listened to the pastor speak on giving to others. Later that night, Margie slipped out the back door to look up at the stars. "Thank you," she whispered, "for giving me my wish."

That was just one of the many wishes granted for Margie as she grew up. Margie was truly a blessed little girl. I should know—I was that little girl.

Margaret E. Mack
Chicken Soup for the Golden Soul

𝒯here is no beautifier of complexion or form of behavior like the wish to scatter joy, and not pain, around us.

—Ralph Waldo Emerson

Grandma,
I wish every
family had a
grandmother
as wonderful
as you.

Half-Listened

So many of our friends were becoming grandparents, and we kept hearing, "You're going to love being grandparents. There's nothing like it."

These are the same people who have "Let Me Tell You About My Grandchildren" bumper stickers plastered all over their car bumpers. The same people who refer to themselves as "Evan's grandmaw" or "Ashley's grandpaw."

I didn't doubt for a minute that they relished their roles. But that wasn't for John and me. We were entering the senior citizen's discount stage of our lives, looking forward to the day when we might be able to actually get that motor home and do some traveling. I enjoy my quiet time, and John would truly love nothing more than to be able to wander off to his favorite fishing hole and linger awhile under the shade of a big ol' magnolia tree with a cold adult beverage in hand.

Now we've raised two perfectly beautiful sons for whom the phrase "boys will be boys" was most certainly coined. There are no more messy diapers or cutting teeth or endless nights of worrying when one of them came down with a fever or the chicken pox. We wanted to trade our family car in for a spiffy little two-passenger candy apple red Corvette—no room for a car seat or diaper bags or any of the necessary gear one needs when taking a day trip to Disney.

Then, along comes Quinton—eight pounds, thirteen ounces of pure joy—double dimples and a smile that would melt your heart. A little bit of feistiness that comes from, well, several sources on his daddy's side and a sweetness that is most assuredly a combination of his precious mommy and daddy.

Okay, you pals of mine—you tried to tell us and we half-listened. We never dreamed that the depth of love we could feel for such a tiny human being could run so deeply. Or that we can hardly wait to hear the phone ring and to be asked, "Can you come over and watch Quinton while we eat?"

Holding that sweet little bundle brings a sense of calm over me, the likes of which I can hardly believe. Even if he's having a fussy spell, I still marvel at the softness of his features, the smell of that oh-so-soft baby skin. So, maybe I'll just get used to the fact that my graying hair and wrinkled skin qualifies me for the role of someone's grandmother.

Now, will someone please tell me where I can buy one of those silly "Let Me Tell You About My Grandchildren" bumper stickers?

Debby Stoner
Chicken Soup for the Grandparent's Soul

If I had known how wonderful it would be to have grandchildren, I'd have had them first.

—Lois Wyse

Grandma,
your smiles are
like sunshine on
a rainy day.

Second Chance

When they were small and I was young,
I often had no time for fun.

There was cleaning to do and bills to pay.
I rushed upon my busy way.

And when I tucked them in to sleep,
I'd obligations still to keep.

I kissed them, and I turned away
My promises broken another day.

We had good times. I loved them dear,
But interruptions grew each year.

Then suddenly, they'd grown and gone.
I felt like life's discarded pawn.

But then, a miracle. It's true.
This time I recognized my cue,

And let each precious moment be
Embraced and savored happily.

My children's children now I see,
Gathered sweetly at my knee.

I send an upward, grateful glance,
That God gave me a second chance.

L. D. Hindman
Chicken Soup for the Mother's Soul 2

A Grandma Takes Power

When my grandmother was eighty-nine years old she was having problems with her heart. My family went with her to the cardiologist who told her that she had a serious heart condition that required surgery. However, the eminent physician warned that because of my grandmother's age, complications could arise. He went on to say that because of her age, my grandmother would have a 40 percent chance of having a heart attack during the operation, a 35 percent chance of having a stroke, a 30 percent chance of dying on the operating room table . . .

My grandmother, shocked, quickly interrupted the doctor and said, "Doctor, as long as you're talking about statistics, I have one for you: THERE'S A 100 percent CHANCE OF YOU NOT OPERATING ON ME!" With these words, my grandmother got up and left the doctor's office.

My grandmother might be stubborn, but she's no fool. So the next day she went to another doctor where he, too, told her she needed surgery. He also stated that her age might cause a problem, BUT he was telling her in a way that was positive as opposed to the negative way of the previous day.

My grandmother then asked the doctor, "If I were your mother, what would you recommend?"

The doctor walked up to her, smiled, put his arm around her, and said, "Mom, let's have the operation!"

She had the operation and came out fine! Her positive

attitude (which is vital to her and everyone) added many wonderful, happy years to enjoy life and her family.

Michael Jordan Segal
Chicken Soup for the Grandparent's Soul

Two Dedicated Grandmas

Who would have ever imagined they'd do such a thing?

Joel, my son, was celebrating his fourth birthday. Our family and friends gathered at the local Discovery Zone to party. After pizza and presents, it was time to play.

The kids crawled into the ball pen, where they literally swam through hundreds of balls. A large tunnel wound up and around the building. One by one, children crawled up and through the tunnel and traveled down its slide, shooting out the end straight into the sea of balls.

I never saw them make their move, finding their way into the balls. I didn't even see them enter the tunnel that climbed up to the top of the slide.

But I heard them!

My head turned. *It couldn't be . . . they couldn't have!*

But they had!

My jaw dropped as I looked up and saw Grandma Mary Lou and Grandma Joyce on all fours, cramped inside the tunnel at the top of the slide.

"You go first," Grandma Mary Lou insisted.

"Well, I have to!" Grandma Joyce replied. "You couldn't get around me if you wanted too!"

And then giggles and laughter, like that of schoolgirls, streamed out of the tunnel . . . but no grandmas followed.

I maneuvered closer and positioned my camera, getting the perfect picture of two dedicated grandmas in ever-so-compromising positions.

"Are you gonna go?" I asked while looking up the tube. "You two are holding up the line."

Within seconds, Grandma Joyce made a splash as she flew down and out the tunnel and was buried beneath the balls.

"Are you okay? Lady, are you okay," a bystander asked.

I held my post and looked up into the tunnel again. Instead of shwooshing down the slide as Grandma Joyce did, Grandma Mary Lou sought a more sophisticated way. With her appendages spread-eagled and securely pressed against the sides of the tunnel, she sought to inch her way down the slide. Her body shook with laughter. Several children, strangers and family members, stood watching to see the last grandma propel from the slide. Wanting to savor the moment, I took more pictures of Grandma Joyce wading through balls and Grandma Mary Lou struggling to maintain somewhat of a ladylike position while contorting down the slide.

Within minutes, two grandmas emerged from the ball pen. Immediately, they headed directly to the little girls room, no doubt to gather their senses and pull themselves together. I marveled at them as they passed me. Grandma Mary Lou and Grandma Joyce, truly two dedicated grandmas—and certainly the life of the party!

Janet Lynn Mitchell
Chicken Soup for the Grandma's Soul

125

Greek Honey Cake

INGREDIENTS:

1 cup all-purpose flour
1½ teaspoons baking
  powder
¼ teaspoon salt
½ teaspoon cinnamon
2 teaspoon orange zest
¾ cup butter
¾ cup white sugar

3 eggs
¼ cup milk
1 cup chopped walnuts

1 cup white sugar
1 cup honey
¾ cup water
1 teaspoon lemon juice

DIRECTIONS:

Preheat oven to 350 Grease and flour a 9 inch cake pan.

In a bowl, combine the flour, baking powder, salt, cinnamon and orange rind. Set aside.

In another large bowl, cream together the butter and ¾ cup sugar until light and fluffy.

One at a time, beat in the eggs and add the orange zest.

Mix in the dry ingredients alternating with the milk just until incorporated.

Stir in the walnuts.

Pour batter into prepared pan and bake for 40 minutes, or until a toothpick inserted into the center of the cake comes out clean. Allow to cool for 15 minutes and cut the cake into diamond shapes.

HONEY SYRUP:

In a saucepan, combine honey, 1 cup of sugar and water. Bring to a simmer and cook for 5 minutes, constantly stirring. Stir in lemon juice, bring to a boil and cook for 2 minutes.

Pour honey syrup over the cake.

The Origins of Mother's Day

The earliest version of Mother's day was in ancient Greece where, in the springtime, people celebrated the goddess, Rhea, who was the mother of all gods. At dawn they would offer her honey cakes, fine drinks and flowers.

About the Authors

Who Is Jack Canfield?

Jack Canfield is one of America's leading experts in the development of human potential and personal effectiveness. He is both a dynamic, entertaining speaker and a highly sought-after trainer. Jack has a wonderful ability to inform and inspire audiences toward increased levels of self-esteem and peak performance. He has authored or coauthored numerous books, including *Dare to Win, The Aladdin Factor, 100 Ways to Build Self-Concept in the Classroom, Heart at Work* and *The Power of Focus*. His latest book is *The Success Principles*.

www.jackcanfield.com

Who is Mark Victor Hansen?

In the area of human potential, no one is more respected than **Mark Victor Hansen**. For more than thirty years, Mark has focused solely on helping people from all walks of life reshape their personal vision of what's possible. His powerful messages of possibility, opportunity and action have created powerful change in thousands of organizations and millions of individuals worldwide. He is a prolific writer of bestselling books such as *The One Minute Millionaire, The Power of Focus, The Aladdin Factor* and *Dare to Win*.

www.markvictorhansen.com

Contributors

Nadia Ali is an experienced freelance writer. She resides on the Caribbean island of Trinidad with her husband, Khaleel, and two daughters, Shazara and Raisah, who were the inspiration for this humorous story about their grandmother, Azmine Khan. Nadia can be reached at *nadia@freelance-worker.com*.

Linda Apple lives in northwest Arkansas with her husband, Neal, their five children and two grandchildren. She is a speaker for Stonecroft Ministries and contributor to *Chicken Soup for the Nurse's Soul, Chicken Soup for the Working Woman's Soul* and *Chicken Soup for the Soul Living Your Dreams*. Contact Linda at *Psalm10218@cox-internet.com* or *www.lindacapple.com*.

Ellie Braun-Haley is the author of four books. She also has short stories published in *Chicken Soup for the Soul*, other books and a wide variety of online e-zines. She presents workshops to kindergarten teachers and others in creative dance and movement for children. Please e-mail her at *shaley@telusplanet.net*.

Alice Collins and her husband, John, have been blessed and perplexed by four fine sons and one lovely daughter. The aggravation was worth it all because now they have ten wonderful grandchildren to spoil! Alice, a professional speaker, writes two weekly columns filled with the sentiment and humor of family life.

Angela D'Valentine is a native Californian. She loves children, dogs and houseplants—and as she frequently tells her loving husband, Matthew, she might write more if she had a larger computer monitor, though he thinks all she needs is a trip to the optometrist.

Nancy B. Gibbs is a pastor's wife, mother and grandmother. She is also an author, weekly religion columnist and freelance writer. Her stories have appeared in *Chicken Soup for the Nurse's Soul, Stories* *for the Heart, Honor Books, Guideposts Books, Chocolate for Women and Heartwarmer's, Angels on Earth, Family Circle, Woman's World, Decision, Happiness* and *Georgia Magazine.* Nancy may be contacted at *Daiseydood@aol.com.*

Bonnie S. Grau is a freelance writer who enjoys reading, cooking, traveling and spending time with her three young grandchildren. She and her husband live in York, Pennsylvania.

L. D. Hindman is a grandmother whose avocation is writing poetry. She recently completed a small volume of verse, *Among Stones,* written to bring comfort to those who have experienced the loss of a loved one. She lives in Colorado with her husband of thirty-eight years, where she enjoys all activities that involve her family.

Mary Ann Horenstein received a B.A. degree from Smith College and a master's and doctorate from Rutgers University. She taught English, then headed an experiential learning program in a New Jersey school before retiring. She has published two books and many articles. She can be reached at *madon@surfglobal.net.*

Maryann Lee Jacob is a psychology teacher at Stevens High School in Rapid City, South Dakota. She has several poems published in South Dakota's *Prairie Winds.* She also has a college grammar book published entitled *Fundamentals of English.* She has five children and can be reached at 3304 Idlewild Court, Rapid City, SD or call 605-341-2843.

Kathryn Kimzey Judkins, LVN, has lived in California since 1962. Since retiring in 1998, she spends much of her time writing poetry and short stories. Married fifty-eight years, she has three children, six grandchildren and three great-grandchildren.

Karren E. Key has a blended family of five children and thirteen beautiful grandchildren. Her husband Lacy's job moves them all over the United States, so they rarely are able to live near any of their family. She is making her special memories of each of them even more special.

Robin Lim is the mother of seven, grandmother of "Zhou" and midwife of many. She lives with her large family in the mountains of the Philippines, and can sometimes be found in Iowa. Her book, *After the Baby's Birth: A Woman's Way to Wellness*, is a wonderful guidebook for new mothers. Lim is director of Healthy Mother—Healthy Baby, an international not-for-profit foundation that supports gentle, culturally sensitive childbirth and breastfeeding. Donations may be sent to HEALTHY MOTHER—HEALTHY BABY, 4286 Redwood Hwy., #330, San Rafael, CA 94930.

Margaret E. Mack is author of three books, including one of poetry. Currently attending law school, Margie is married and has four grown sons. She was reared in Illinois with her grandparents; she considers them to be "my best friends."

Patricia S. Mays is a tremendous fan of the ordinary person and has a special ability to see humor in "life as usual" events. Born in a small town in Idaho, Patti is a member of a large family that loves to laugh. She has had previous stories published, including one in the "Life in These United States" section of *Reader's Digest*. Patti, husband John and daughter Natalie live in Atlanta, Georgia.

Terri McPherson lives in Windsor, Ontario, Canada, with her husband, Ray. She is the mother of two adult children, and a grandmother to the one and only Caitlynd. As the editor and contributing writer of an online newsletter, she writes about the small human threads that connect us to one another. She can be reached at tmcphers@mnsi.net.

Janet Lynn Mitchell is a wife, mother, author and inspirational speaker. She is the coauthor of A Special Kind of Love, For Those Who Love Children with Special Needs, published by Broadman and Holman and Focus on the Family, 2004. Janet can be reached at *Janetlm@prodigy.net* or by fax (714) 633-6309.

Wanda Mitchell is a wife, mother and grandmother residing in Alta Loma, California. She works as a librarian aide for Etiwanda Intermediate School. She is also a travel agent, specializing in cruises. Her passions include her family, reading, writing and seeing the world from a cruise ship. You may contact her at *Travel980@aol.com*.

Cassie Moore enjoys being a full-time mom to her son Brady. She likes to read, write poems and short stories, and spend time with her family and friends. She wrote "The Magic Jar Years" in memory of her mom, Gloria, who continues to be her inspiration from above. Cassie, her husband Scott, and Brady reside in Spanish Fort, Alabama. You can e-mail her at *cbsmoore@att.net*.

Doris Hays Northstrom is a nationally published author, inspirational speaker and creative-writing teacher, and acquires material from family, friends, forest, pets, solitude, books, biking and gardening. She has four children and five grandchildren, adding five more grandchildren to love since marrying Ron in December 1998. Write her at 1308 N. Cascade Ave., Tacoma, WA 98406 or call 253-759-9829.

Linda Osmundson is a freelance writer, former teacher and art docent in four art museums—Phoenix, Utah, Denver and Seattle. She lives in Ft. Collins, Colorado, with her husband of thirty-six years. She enjoys crafts, golf, writing, reading and grandparenting. You may reach her at *LLO1413@aol.com*.

Carol McAdoo Rehme, one of *Chicken Soup's* managing editors and most prolific contributors, compares grannyhood to homemade happiness—life's natural sweetener. Carol directs a nonprofit organization, Vintage Voices, Inc., which brings interactive programming to the vulnerable elderly. Speaking engagements and storytelling gigs fill her spare time. Contact her at *carol@rehme.com* or *www.rehme.com*.

Stephen D. Rogers is a stay-at-home dad who is late with his own thank-you notes. Please e-mail him at *sdr633@hotmail.com*.

Kathy Ryan is a widowed mother of four children. She is the director of social ministries and family life in a parish on Long Island. Kathy's work includes a ministry to young moms, bereaved people, and those divorced and separated. She uses storytelling as a vehicle for growth and healing in all her Family Life Programs.

Michael Jordan Segal is a social worker at Memorial Hermann Hospital in Houston, Texas, an author, and an inspirational/motivational speaker. His "miraculous comeback" story has been featured on national television and magazines. Mike's story, "My Miraculous Family," was published in *Chicken Soup for the Christian Family Soul*. He is available for public-speaking engagements and can be reached via e-mail at *MsegalHope@aol.com*.

Debby Stoner lives happily in the Sunshine State with her husband and pets. Her two wonderful grown sons live close by. She spends her days taking care of Quinton, who at the age of eight months, has given new meaning to the words "perfect love."

LeAnn Thieman is an author and nationally acclaimed speaker, inspiring audiences to make a difference in the world. She coauthored *This Must Be My Brother*, recounting her role in the rescue of three hundred babies during the Vietnam Orphan airlift. She can be contacted at 112 North College, Fort Collins, CO 80524, toll-free 877-THIEMAN, or at *www.LeAnnThieman.com*. LeAnn also coauthored *Chicken Soup for the Nurse's Soul*.

Diane M. Vanover writes from her home in Tucson, Arizona, where she shares her love of stories with her five terrific grandchildren: Travis,

David, Amanda, Alexis and Mishelle, who are superb and inspirational storytellers. You may contact her at *dmvanover@aol.com*.

Lynne Zielinski is "Nana" to thirteen grandkids in Huntsville, Alabama, and believes all children are a gift from God. Thrilled when a teenager seeks her advice, Lynne is astounded when they heed it. She writes inspirational stories, short fiction and enjoys freelance work. E-mail her at *Excell1047@aol.com*.

Permissions